Table of Contents

DAY TRADING 2021

Chapter One

Understanding Day Trading

Day trading is the demonstration of purchasing and selling a money related instrument around the same time or even on various occasions through the span of a day. Exploiting little value moves can be a rewarding game—on the off chance that it is played accurately. However, it very well may be a risky game for amateurs or any individual who doesn't stick to a well-considered system. In addition, not all merchants are appropriate for the high volume of trades made by day traders. A few traders, be that as it may, are planned in view of the day trader.

How about we investigate some broad day trading standards and afterward proceed onward to choosing when to purchase and sell, regular day trading procedures, fundamental diagrams, and examples, and how to restrict misfortunes.

Day Trading Strategies

1. Information Is Power

Notwithstanding information on essential exchanging systems, day traders need to keep up on the most recent securities exchange news and occasions that influence stocks—the Fed's financing cost designs, the monetary standpoint, and so on. So get your work done. Make a list of things to get an idea of stocks you'd prefer to trade and keep yourself educated about the chose organizations and general markets. Output business news and visit dependable money related sites.

2. Put Aside Funds

Do a proper evaluation of how much capital you're willing to hazard on each trade. Numerous fruitful day traders chance under 1% to 2% of their record per trade. In the event that you have a $40,000 trading account and are eager to chance 0.5%

of your capital on each trade, your most extreme loss per trade is $200 (0.005 x $40,000). Put aside a surplus measure of assets you can exchange with, and you're set up to lose. Keep in mind; it could possibly occur.

3. Put Aside Time, Too

Day trading requires your time. That is the reason it's called day trading. You'll have to surrender the vast majority of your day, truth be told. Try not to think of it as in the event that you have restricted time to save. The procedure requires a broker to follow the business sectors and spot openings, which can emerge whenever during trading hours. Moving rapidly is critical.

4. Start Small

As a learner, center around a limit of one to two stocks during a session. Following and discovering openings is simpler, with only a couple of stocks.

As of late, it has gotten progressively normal to have the option to trade fragmentary offers, so you can determine explicitly, littler dollar sums you wish to contribute. That implies if Apple shares are trading at $250 and you just need to purchase $50 worth, numerous representatives will currently let you buy one-fifth of an offer.

5. Stay away from Penny Stocks

You're most likely searching at arrangements and low costs, yet avoid penny stocks. These stocks are regularly illiquid, and the odds of hitting a big stake are frequently somber. Numerous stocks trading under $5 an offer become de-recorded from significant stock trades and are just tradable over-the-counter (OTC). Except if you see a genuine chance and have done your examination, avoid these.

6. Time Those Trades

Numerous requests set by investors and brokers start to execute when the business sectors open in the first part of the day, which adds to value instability. A prepared player might have the option to perceive examples and pick fittingly to make benefits. Be that as it may, for beginners, it might be better just to peruse the market without making any moves for the initial 15 to 20 minutes. The center hours are typically less unpredictable, and afterward, development starts to get again toward the end ringer. Despite the fact that the times of heavy traffic offer chances, it's more secure for amateurs to maintain a strategic distance from them from the start.

7. Cut Losses With Limit Orders

Choose what kind of orders you'll use to enter and leave trades. Will you use showcase requests or farthest point orders? At the point when you put in a market request, it's executed at the best value accessible at the time—hence, no value ensures.

A cutoff request, then, ensures the cost, however, not the execution. Farthest point orders assist you with trading with more accuracy, wherein you set your cost (not ridiculous but rather executable) for purchasing just like selling. Progressively advanced and experienced informal investors may utilize the utilization of alternatives methodologies to support their situations also.

8. Be Realistic About Profits

A system doesn't have to win constantly to be productive. Plenty traders just win half to 60% of their trades. In any case, they make more on their victors than they lose on their washouts. Ensure the hazard on each trade is constrained to a particular level of the record, and that section and leave techniques are unmistakably characterized and recorded.

9. Remain Cool

There are times when the securities trades test your nerves. As a day trader, you have to figure out how to keep ravenousness, expectation, and dread under control. Choices ought to be represented by rationale and not feeling.

10. Stay on track

Effective brokers need to move quickly, yet they don't need to think quick. Why? Since they've built up a trading procedure advance, alongside the control to adhere to that system. It is critical to pursue your recipe intently as opposed to attempt to pursue benefits. Try not to let your feelings defeat you and relinquish your methodology. There's a mantra among day traders: "Plan your trade and trade your plan."

Before we go into a portion of the intricate details of day trading, how about, we take a look at a portion of the reasons why day trading can be so troublesome.

What Makes Day Trading Difficult?

Day trading takes a ton of training and ability, and there are a few factors that can make the procedure testing.

To start with, realize that you're going toward experts whose vocations rotate around trading. These individuals approach the best innovation and associations in the business, so regardless of whether they come up short, they're set up to prevail at last. In the event that you get on board with the temporary fad, it implies more benefits for them.

Uncle Sam will likewise need a cut of your benefits, regardless of how thin. Recollect that you'll need to pay assesses on any transient additions—or any ventures you hold for one year or less—at the negligible rate. The one admonition is that your misfortunes will balance any additions.

As an individual financial specialist, you might be inclined to enthusiastic and mental inclinations. Proficient brokers are typically ready to remove these of their exchanging methodologies, yet when it's your own capital included, it will, in general, be an alternate story.

Choosing What and When to Buy

Day traders attempt to make cash by abusing minute value developments in singular resources (stocks, monetary standards, prospects, and alternatives), typically utilizing a lot of money to do as such. In choosing what to concentrate on—in a stock, say—a run of the mill day trader searches for three things:

Liquidity: Liquidity enables you to enter and leave a stock at a decent cost. For example, tight spreads or the contrast between the offer and solicit cost from stock, and low slippage or the distinction between the normal cost of exchange and the real cost.

Unpredictability: Volatility is essentially a proportion of the normal everyday value extend—the range wherein an informal investor works. Greater unpredictability implies more prominent benefit or misfortune.

Trading volume: This is a proportion of how often stock is purchased and sold in a given time span—most ordinarily known as the normal day by day exchanging volume. A high level of volume demonstrates a great deal of enthusiasm for a stock. Expansion in a stock's volume is frequently a harbinger of a value bounce, either up or down.

When you recognize what sort of stocks (or different resources) you're searching for, you have to figure out how to distinguish section focuses—that is, at what exact minute you will contribute. Devices that can assist you in doing this include:

Constant news administrations: News moves stocks, so it's critical to buy into administrations that disclose to you when possibly showcase moving news turns out.

ECN/Level 2 statements: ECNs, or electronic correspondence systems, are PC based frameworks that show the best accessible offer and ask cites from various market members and afterward naturally coordinate and execute orders. Level 2 is a membership-based help that gives ongoing access to the Nasdaq request book made out of value cites from market producers enlisting each Nasdaq-recorded and OTC Bulletin Board security. Together, they can give you a feeling of requests being executed continuously.

Intraday candle outlines: Candlesticks give a crude examination of value activity. More on these later.

Characterize and record the conditions under which you'll enter a position. "Purchase during upturn" isn't sufficiently explicit. Something like this is considerably more explicit and furthermore testable: "Purchase when value breaks over the upper trendline of a triangle design, where the triangle was gone before by an upturn (in any event one higher swing highs and higher swing low before the triangle framed) on the two-minute diagram in the initial two hours of the exchanging day."

When you have a particular arrangement of section rules, filter through more graphs to check whether those conditions are created every day (accepting you need to day trade each day) and, as a rule, produce a value move the foreseen way. Assuming this is the case, you have a potential passage point for a system. You'll at that point need to evaluate how to exit, or sell, those trades.

Choosing When to Sell

There are different approaches to leave a triumphant position, including trailing stops and benefit targets. Benefit targets are the most widely recognized leave technique, taking a benefit at a pre-decided level.

Day Trading Charts and Patterns

To help decide the perfect minute to purchase a stock (or anything that benefit you're exchanging), numerous merchants use:

- Candle designs, including inundating candles and dojis

- Specialized analysis, including pattern lines and triangles

Volume—expanding or diminishing

There are numerous candle arrangements a day trader can search for to discover a section point. Whenever utilized appropriately, the doji inversion design (featured in yellow in the graph underneath) is one of the most solid ones.

Day Trading Patterns

Commonly, search for an example like this with a few affirmations:

To begin with, search for a volume spike, which will give you whether traders are supporting the cost at this level. Note: this can be either on the doji light or on the candles promptly tailing it.

Second, search for earlier help at this value level — for instance, the earlier low of day (LOD) or high of day (HOD).

At long last, take a look at the Level 2 circumstance, which will show all the open requests and request sizes.

In the event that you pursue these three stages, you can decide if the doji is probably going to deliver a genuine turnaround and can take a position if the conditions are good.

Conventional examination of graph designs additionally gives benefit focuses to exits. For instance, the stature of a triangle at the most extensive part is added to the breakout purpose of the triangle (for an upside breakout), giving a cost at which to take benefits.

The Most Effective Method To Limit Losses When Day Trading

A stop-loss request is intended to confine losses on a situation in a security. For long positions, a stop loss can be put beneath an ongoing low, or for short positions, over an ongoing high. It can likewise be founded on unpredictability. For instance, on the off chance that stock value is moving about $0.05 per minute, at that point, you may put a prevent loss $0.15 away from your entrance to give the value some space to change before it moves your foreseen way.

Characterize precisely how you'll control the risk on the trades. On account of a triangle design, for example, a stop loss can be set $0.02 beneath an ongoing swing low if purchasing a breakout, or $0.02 underneath the example. (The $0.02 is subjective; the fact is just to be explicit.)

One procedure is to set two stop loss:

A physical stop-loss request put at a specific value level that suits your hazard resilience. Basically, this is the most cash you can remain to lose.

A psychological stop-loss set at where your entrance criteria are abused. This implies if the trade makes a surprising turn, you'll quickly leave your position.

Any way you choose to leave your trades, the leave criteria must be sufficiently explicit to be testable and repeatable. Likewise, it's critical to set a most extreme misfortune for every day you can stand to withstand—both monetarily and rationally. At whatever point you hit this point, take the remainder of a vacation day.

Adhere to your arrangement and your borders. All things considered, tomorrow is another (trading) day.

When you've characterized how you enter trades and where you'll put a stop misfortune, you can survey whether the potential system fits inside your hazard limit. On the off chance that the procedure uncovered you an excessive amount of hazard, you have to change the system here and there to decrease the hazard.

In the event that the procedure is inside your hazard limit, at that point, testing starts. Physically experience verifiable outlines to discover your entrances, taking note of whether your stop loss or target would have been hit. Paper trade along these lines for at any rate 50 to 100 trades, taking note of whether the procedure was gainful and on the off chance that it lives up to your desires. On the off chance that it does, continue to trading the system of a demo account progressively. On the off chance that it's beneficial through the span of two months or more in a mimicked domain, continue with day exchanging the methodology with genuine capital. In the event that the procedure isn't productive, begin once again.

At long last, remember that if trading on margin—which means you're getting your venture assets from a financier firm (and remember that margin prerequisite for day trading are high)— you're unquestionably progressively defenseless against sharp value developments. Margin enhances the trading results of benefits, yet of losses also if trade conflicts with you. Thusly, utilizing stop losses is pivotal when day trading on margin.

Chapter Two

Contrasts Between Day Trading and Swing Trading

The time span on which a trader selects to trade can significantly affect the trading system and benefit. Day traders open and close numerous positions inside a solitary day, while swing merchants take trades that last several days, weeks, or even months. These two diverse trading styles can suit different brokers relying upon the measure of capital accessible, time accessibility, brain science, and the market being traded.

One trading style isn't superior to the other, and it truly comes down to which style suits a trader's close to home conditions. A few brokers select to do either, while others might be day traders, swing traders and purchase and-hold investors at the same time.

Potential Returns

Day trading pulls in traders searching for a fast exacerbating of profits. Assume a broker risks 0.5% of their capital on each exchange. In the event that they lose, they shall lose 0.5%, yet in the event that they win, they'll make 1% (2:1 reward to risk proportion).

Additionally, assume they win half of their trades. On the off chance that they make six trades for every day, by and large, they will add about 1.5% to their record balance every day, minus trading expenses. Earning at least 1% a day would grow a trading account by over 200% throughout the year, uncompounded.

On the other side, while the numbers appear to be anything but difficult to repeat for enormous returns, nothing's ever that simple. Making twice as much on wins as you lost on failures, while additionally winning half of the considerable number of trades you take, doesn't come easily. You can make brisk increases, yet you can likewise quickly drain your trading account through day trading.

Swing trading gathers additions and misfortunes more gradually than day trading. However you can, in any case, have certain swing trades that rapidly bring about large gains or losses. Assume a swing trader utilizes a similar risk management rule and risks 0.5% of their capital on each trade with the objective of attempting to make 1% to 2% on their triumphant trades.

Assume they acquire 1.5% by and large for winning exchanges, losing 0.5% on losing exchanges. They make six exchanges for every month and win half of those exchanges. In a common month, the swing trader could add 3% to their account balance, minus expenses. Through the span of the year, that turns out to about 36%, which sounds great;

however, offers less potential than a day trader's conceivable profit.

These model situations serve to outline the difference between the two trading styles. Adjusting the level of trades won, the normal win contrasted with normal loss, or the number of trades, will definitely influence a procedure's procuring potential.

When in doubt, day trading has more benefit potential, in any event on littler accounts. As the size of the account develops, it gets increasingly hard to use all the capital on exceptionally transient day trades viably.

Day traders may discover their rate returns decrease the more capital they have. Their dollar returns may, in any case, go up, since making 5% on $1 million compares to significantly more than 20% on $100,000. Swing traders have less possibility of this occurrence.

Fluctuating Capital Necessities

Capital necessities fluctuate as per the market being traded. Day traders and swing traders can begin with varying measures of capital relying upon whether they trade in the stock, forex, or futures markets .

In places like the United States of America, Day trading stocks requires an account balance of at any rate $25,000. No lawful minimum exists to swing trade stocks, albeit a swing trader will probably need to have at any rate $10,000 in their account, and ideally $20,000 if hoping to draw a salary from trading.

To day trade the forex market, no lawful minimum exists, yet it is prescribed that traders start with at least $500, yet ideally $1,000 or more. To swing trade forex, the base suggested is about $1,500, however ideally more. This measure of capital will enable you to enter at any rate a couple of trades one after another.

To day trade futures, start with at any rate $5,000 to $7,500, and increasing capital would be far and more superior. These sums rely upon the prospects contract being exchanged. With day trading, a few agreements could require substantially more capital, while a couple of agreements, for example, miniaturized scale contracts, may require less.

To swing trade an assortment of futures contracts, you need at any rate $10,000, and likely $20,000 or more. The sum required relies upon the margin prerequisites of the particular contract being traded.

Time for Trading Differs

Both types of trading need a measure of time investment, yet day trading commonly occupies significantly more time. Day traders as a rule trade for in any event two hours out of each day. Including planning time and chart/trading audit implies spending at any rate three to four hours at the PC, at any rate. In the event that a day trader selects to trade for in excess of several hours per day, the time venture goes up impressively, and it turns into an all-day work.

Swing trading, then again, can take considerably less time. For instance, in case you're swing trading off a day by day chart, you could discover new trades and update orders on current situations in around 45 minutes every night. These exercises may not be required on a daily premise.

Some traders who engage in swing trading, taking trades that last weeks or months, may just need to search for trades and update orders once every week, bringing the time responsibility down to about an hour out of every week rather than every night, or refreshing orders may not be required on a daily premise.

You should likewise do day trading while a market is open and dynamic. The best hours for day trading are constrained to specific times of the day. In the event that you can't day trade during those hours, at that point, pick swing trading as a superior alternative. Swing traders can search for trades or spot orders whenever in the day, significantly after the market has shut.

Swing traders are less influenced continuously to-second changes in the cost of an advantage. They center around the master plan, normally seeing day by day charts, so setting trades after the market closes on a specific day works fine and dandy. Day traders make cash off second-by-second developments, so they should be included while the activity is going on.

Focus, Time, and Practice

Day trading and Swing trading both require a decent arrangement of work and information to create benefits reliably, despite the fact that the information required isn't really "book smarts." Successful trading comes about because of finding a methodology that delivers an edge, or a benefit over a noteworthy number of trades, and afterward executing that technique again and again.

Some information available being traded and one beneficial procedure can begin creating pay, alongside parts and bunches of training. Everyday costs move uniquely in contrast to they did on the last, which implies the broker should have the option to actualize their procedure under different conditions and adjust as conditions change.

This shows a troublesome test, and predictable outcomes just originate from rehearsing a methodology under heaps of various market situations. That requires some serious energy and ought to include making many trades a demo account before gambling real capital.

Picking day trading or swing trading likewise comes down to character. Day trading ordinarily includes more pressure, requires continued concentration for expanded timeframes, and takes mind-boggling discipline. Individuals that like activity, have quick reflexes, and additionally like computer games and poker will in general incline toward day trading.

Swing trading occurs at a more slow pace, with any longer slips between activities like entering or leaving trades. It can even now be high pressure, and furthermore requires tremendous order and tolerance.

It doesn't require as much focus, so on the off chance that you experience issues remaining focused, swing trading might be the better alternative. Quick reflexes don't make a difference in swing trading as trades can be taken after the market closes, and prices have quit moving.

Swing trading and day trading both offer freedom in the sense that a broker works for themselves. Brokers commonly take a shot at their own, and they are liable for subsidizing their accounts and for all losses and benefits created. One can contend that swing traders have more opportunity as far as time since swing trading occupies less time than day exchanging.

A Final Comparison

One trading style isn't superior to the next; they simply suit varying needs. Day trading has more benefit potential, in any event in rate terms on littler estimated trading accounts. Swing traders have a superior possibility of keeping up their rate returns even as their account develops, in a specific way.

Capital prerequisites fluctuate a considerable amount over the various markets and trading styles. Day trading requires additional time than swing trading, while both take a lot of training to pick up consistency. Day training makes the best alternative for activity lovers. Those looking for a lower-push and less time-escalated choice can grasp swing trading.

Chapter Three

Day Trading Upsides and Downsides

Upsides

1. Potential to make considerable benefits: The greatest bait of day trading is the potential for terrific benefits. Be that as it may, this may just be a likelihood for the uncommon person who has every one of the qualities – definitiveness, discipline, and perseverance – required to turn into a fruitful day trader.

2. Work for yourself: The day trader works alone, autonomous from the impulses of corporate fat cats. He can have an adaptable working timetable, get some much-needed rest at whatever point required, and work at his own pace, in contrast to somebody on the corporate treadmill.

3. A constant flood of excitement: Long-time day traders love the rush of setting their brains in opposition to the market and different experts throughout each and every day. The adrenaline surge from fast fire trading is something that relatively few brokers will admit to, yet is a major factor in their choice to bring home the bacon from trading, contrasted, and going through their days selling gadgets or poring over numbers in an office work area.

4. Costly training not required: For some occupations in finances, having the correct degree from the correct college is essential only for a meeting. Day trading, interestingly, doesn't require costly instruction from an Ivy League school. While there are no formal instructive necessities for turning into a day trader, courses in specialized analysis and digital trading might be useful.

5. Independent work benefits: As an independently employed individual, a day trader can discount certain costs for tax purposes, which can't be guaranteed by an employed person.

Downsides

1. The danger of considerable loses: One major truth about day trading is that day traders regularly endure monetary losses in their first long stretches of trading, and numerous never graduate to benefit making status. While the many investment and stockbroking platforms advice that day traders should just hazard cash they can bear to lose. Actually, numerous day traders incur immense losses on monies they borrowed, either through margined trades or capital acquired from family or different sources. These losses may reduce their day trading profession, and additionally put them in considerable debt.

2. Huge beginning and progressing costs: Day traders need to contend with high-recurrence brokers, hedge funds, and other market experts who burn through millions to pick up trading points of interest. In this condition, a day trader has a minimal decision but to spend intensely on a charting software, trading platform, best model PCs, and so forth.

Continuous costs incorporate expenses for getting live cost statements and commission costs that can accrue due to the volume of trades.

3. Work for yourself: To truly make a to go at it, a trader must stop his normal everyday employment and surrender his consistent, regularly scheduled salary. From that point on, the informal investor must depend altogether alone on expertise and endeavors to produce enough benefit to take care of the tabs and appreciate an okay way of life.

4. High pressure and danger of burnout: Day trading is stressful as a direct result of the need to watch numerous screens to spot trading openings and afterward act rapidly to make optimal use of them. This has to be done daily without missing a single day, and the prerequisite for such a high level of concentration and fixation can frequently prompt burnout.

Chapter Four

Day Trading Strategies the Pros Don't Want You to Know

Day trading is quick-paced. It requires an order and exceptionally quick reflexes to pull the trigger once a promising trading opportunity uncovers. It very well may be a lucrative and energizing exchanging style in the event that you get the establishments right.

That is the reason we've made a rundown of multi-day trading tips to stay by. From risk management to trend following, pursue these focuses and see your main concern developing.

1. Get ready for your trading day

As a day trader, readiness is one of the most significant undertakings you should begin your day with. This incorporates not just examining the market for potential trade arrangements yet additionally mental and physical readiness and exercise.

Set your alert promptly toward the beginning of the day, so you can have the opportunity to do some short extending activities and prepare for the exchanging day. Before the financial trade opening ringer or the start of the Forex session, look through your outlines and see whether there are some potential exchange arrangements that are in accordance with your trading procedure.

Numerous day traders check the market late at night to plan for the accompanying trading day, which can likewise be a compelling methodology in case you're a night owl.

2. Investigate the principal trading hour

The main trading hour of any monetary market uncovers a ton about the present trading day. Pending requests that were put by traders the day preceding get executed in the initial couple of moments of the new trading day, which can give important knowledge into where the market is going.

Forex traders frequently pursue the value activity of the early trading session to get a feel of the market beat. In the event that there're huge breakout candles, this frequently establishes the pace for the rest of the day. Similar remains constant for stock dealers – feel the market notion by hanging tight for the initial 1-hour flame of the stock you need to trade.

3. Check a financial schedule

Financial schedules incorporate significant market occasions and reports that can make outrageous unpredictability in the market – and instability is fundamental for day trading. Most of the monetary schedules incorporate the stock or cash that is likely affected by the discharge, the anticipated number (additionally called Street desire), the past number, and the real discharge.

Checking a financial schedule for the most significant market reports planned for the day ought to be a customary piece of your morning readiness schedule. Record or recollect the specific occasions of the discharges to stay away from any horrendous astonishments not far off.

Markets will, in general, be unstable if the genuine number varies from the normal number to a huge degree. Contingent upon your market sees this unpredictability can work either possibly in support of you.

4. Peruse significant market news

While most day traders utilize specialized investigation in their trading, its a well-known fact that basics have a vital impact in monetary markets. Essentials can frame new patterns, invert them, and cause significant help and obstruction levels to break, which makes it critical to pursue market news when day trading.

Numerous brokers go through famous budgetary entryways to remain to-date on showcase news, for example, Bloomberg or Reuters. While you don't need to peruse any news that runs over, realizing what is happening in the market will assist you with your market investigation and produce new trading thoughts.

5. Find oversold and overbought budgetary instruments

The trading techniques of day traders can, as a rule, be gathered into three classes: trend following, breakout trading, and counter-trend trading. Whichever procedure you use, finding and trading overbought and oversold budgetary instruments can have a huge effect on your main concern.

Overbought securities will, in general, tumble to their normal trading range, while oversold securities will in general, ascent to their normal trading range after some time. A well-known device to distinguish protections that trade at those extraordinary levels is the Relative Strength Index, which comes worked in with most mainstream trading stages.

Just apply the RSI to your graph and read its worth – an estimation of beneath 30 shows an oversold economic situation, while an estimation of over 70 flag an overbought economic situation. Abstain from purchasing securities that are overbought and selling securities that are oversold.

6. Take trades in the course of the trend

Trend following is one of the most famous trading systems among day traders for an explanation – it works. Trend following alludes to taking trades only the course of the setup trend. In the event that the present trend is up, search for purchasing openings, and if the momentum trend is down, search for selling openings.

To recognize the present trend, you can utilize a simple peak and trough examination or a specialized marker, for example, the ADX (Average Directional Index). A market in an uptrend shapes back to back higher highs and higher lows, while a downtrend market frames continuous lower lows and lower highs. You'll regularly find that, during an upswing, securities become oversold precisely at the purpose of a crisp higher low, which is the value level at which you ought to consider purchasing the security or money pair.

Essentially, during a downtrend, securities typically get overbought directly at where a new lower high is framing, which flag a potential selling opportunity.

In the event that you have to employ the use of the ADX pointer to recognize and exchange patterns, at that point, follow the estimation of the ADX line. A value beneath 25 shows that the market isn't inclining, a value somewhere in the range of 25 and 50 flag a drifting business sector, while values over 50 sign an extremely solid pattern. Utilize the – DI and

+DI lines to recognize the bearing of the pattern – if the – DI line is over the +DI line, you're managing a downtrend, and if the +DI line is over the – DI line, you're managing an upswing.

7. Counter-trend trades can be unsafe

The contrary way to deal with trend following, counter-trend trading alludes to taking trades the other way of a built uptrend. Counter-trend traders expect to benefit on transient value remedies; for example, they attempt to sell at the highest point of higher highs during an upturn, and to purchase at the base of lower lows during downtrends.

At the point when joined with trend following methodologies, counter-trend trading can make all the more trading open doors for traders. Be that as it may, remember that counter-trend trades are commonly less secure than trades that are taken toward the basic pattern.

8. Have severe risk management systems set up

Without sound risk management rules, even the best trading procedure will, at last, lead to huge losses. Risk management encourages you to assume responsibility for your trades, position sizes, losses and benefits. No single trade ought to be permitted to clear out an enormous bit of your trading account, or you'll make some hard memories attempting to return to earn back the original investment.

For instance, in the event that you lose half of your trading account on a solitary trade or two or three trades , it will take you 100% of profits just to come back to breakeven. That is the reason you ought to break down the potential danger of any trade arrangement, utilize a foreordained risk for every trade, take trades with a sufficiently high reward-to-risk proportion, and adhere to the 6% rule.

9. Continuously risk a fixed level of your trading account on any trade

To avoid losses to gain out of power, you should only risk a fixed level of your trading account on any single trade. The brilliant guideline is to never chance over 2% of your trading account on a trade. Here is an example: in the event that you have a $10,000 account, at that point, you shouldn't risk more than $200 on any single trade. Spot your stop-loss precisely at the value level where your all-out loss for that trade would rise to $200.

While 2% is the most extreme risk you ought to be taking on any single trade, you can lessen this rate if you need to. For traders with bigger trading accounts, it's entirely expected to risk just 1% or even 0.5% of their accounts.

10. Break down the reward-to-risk proportion of potential arrangements

The reward-to-risk proportion of a trade alludes to the potential benefit of the trade divided by its potential loss. For instance, in case you're taking a trade that has a benefit capability of $50, however, you're gambling $100, the prize to-chance proportion of that trade would be 0.5. As it were, you're gambling $2 to pick up $1.

This is a case of an ominous reward-to-risk proportion. You ought to never chance beyond what you can conceivably pick up. The best trade arrangements have a prize to-hazard proportion of in any event 2:1 or significantly more; for example, you're gambling $1 to pick up 2$ or more.

11. Adhere to the 6% rule

While the risk per-trade rule of 2% is intended to secure you against an enormous solitary loss that can cause hopeless harm to your trading account, the 6% rule is intended to ensure you against countless littler losses.

49

This standard says that the most extreme sum you should risk on the entirety of your open trades shouldn't surpass 6% of your trading account size. As an example, on the off chance that you stay by risk for each trade of 2%, the all out number of trades you can have at the same time open would be (3 x 2% = 6%). Be that as it may, in the event that you lessen the risk per-trade to 0.5%, at that point the greatest number of trades you can have at the same time running trips to (12 x 0.5% = 6%).

The 6% rule is an incredible defensive measure against a terrible trading day. Envision the entirety of your open trades betray you and hit stop loss, with the 6% rule you would lose just 6% of your trading account.

12. Utilize pending requests where conceivable

Pending requests incorporate stop and breaking point arranges that become market orders when certain conditions are met. Pending requests are amazingly well known among breakout informal investors.

Essentially put in a pending request above or underneath a potential breakout point, and the pending request will naturally execute a market request once the value comes to the predetermined value level. Along these lines, traders don't need to hold up before their exchanging stages throughout the day to get a breakout trade.

Pending requests can likewise lessen slippage, as they get filled just when the market comes to the pre-indicated cost or don't get filled by any means.

13. Keep a trading diary

Trading diaries are an extraordinary method to improve your day trading abilities whenever utilized the right way. By and large, trading diaries ought to incorporate every one of the trades you've taken before, with their individual section levels, stop-loss, and take-profit levels, purposes behind taking the trade, position sizes and other data you may discover pertinent.

14. Make standard reviews of your trade history

In the event that you're normally keeping a trading diary, at that point, remember to perform reviews of your diary passages now and again. This should be possible once every week or once per month, for instance.

These diary reviews will assist you with recognizing repeating trading botches that have prompted losing trades. Is it a specific chart design that just doesn't work for you? Or, on the other hand, do you place your take-benefits excessively wide and stop-losses excessively tight? A trading diary review will give answers to those and different inquiries.

15. Hang tight for affirmation before entering a trade

Did you discover a trade arrangement worth trading? Everything is in accordance with your trading system, and you've distinguished levels to put your stop-loss and take-profit orders? Fantastic! Be that as it may, before you pull the trigger, hanging tight for affirmation can build your prosperity rate fundamentally.

A trade affirmation alludes to market conduct that affirms your analysis; for example, the value begins to move toward you and demonstrates that your analysis looks right.

Candle patterns are an extraordinary device to affirm a trade. Examples, for example, inundating examples, morning and night stars, dojis, sleds, and pin bars are regularly utilized by day traders to affirm a trade arrangement; lastly, open the exchange.

In case you're trading breakouts, you can likewise hang tight for the end of the breakout candle before going into a trade. This is done to forestall counterfeit breakouts and limit potential losses.

16. Try not to let feelings meddle with your trading choices

Trading dependent on feelings is one of the most well-known slip-ups made by day traders that immensely influence their trading execution. Feelings, for example, dread and ravenousness, cause merchants to allow their misfortunes to run and stop their benefits – the two activities that can do critical harm to your trading account.

How to avoid feelings to meddle with your trading and keep a composed mind? The best arrangement is to have a well-characterized trading plan and just to take trades that line up with your methodology. A total trading plan ought to likewise depict your risk management and section and leave focuses.

It makes an orderly way to deal with trading– one which has a lot bigger pace of achievement than trading dependent on feelings.

17. Continuously use stop-losses

Regardless of whether you are day trading, swing trading or scalping, you should utilize stop-losses arranged trading in the entirety of your trades. Stop-losses counteract huge and erratic losses and have a significant impact on risk management. Without stop-losses, you won't have the option to have an exact risk for every trade or apply the 6% rule.

There are four fundamental kinds of stop-losses: volatility stops, chart stops, percentage stops, and time stops. Out of these four sorts, the chart stops return the best outcomes. Chart stops utilize significant specialized levels in an outline, for example, backing and obstruction zones, to locate the best puts in for stop-misfortune requests.

18. Secure your profits

Perhaps the greatest misstep of day traders is that they don't secure their unrealized profits. At the point when you open a trade and it moves into a productive domain, those profits are as yet not your own. They're unrealized until you close the position either altogether or move your stop-losses over your break-even level. When you do that, unrealized profits become acknowledged and secured.

As a dependable guideline, you ought to secure your profits as your trade arrives at nearer to TP. At the point when the trade arrives at 1/3 of your TP, move the SL to breakeven, and when it arrives at 2/3 of your TP, move the SL to 1/3 of TP.

19. Use trailing stops where conceivable

Another effective method to secure your unrealized profits is by utilizing trailing stops. As their name recommends, trailing stops "trail" the value – with each new value tick in support of you, a trailing stop moves your stop-loss one tick in support of you. Be that as it may, if the new value tick isn't in support of you, your stop-loss will remain at its latest level.

Trailing stops are particularly famous among patterns following day traders. By utilizing trailing stops, they're ready to remain inside a pattern as long as it keeps going and press the most benefits out of it.

20. Try not to trade during significant market reports

Day traders live on instability, and market reports frequently give the vital unpredictability to gainful trades. Without unpredictability, there's no risk and no profits to be made.

Nonetheless, trading during significant market reports can make a situation of pointless risk as business sectors are infamous to make enormous spikes in the seconds following a market release. These spikes frequently lead to a huge broadening of spreads, slippage, and the activating of stop-loss orders.

21. Holding trades medium-term can be unsafe

Day traders are day traders since they hold their exchanges for a solitary day typically– that is it. Most day traders open their trades in the morning and let them run until either their stop-loss or take-profit gets activated.

In the event that an exchange is as yet open before the finish of the trading day, close it and assume the loss of profit. Holding trades medium-term puts you helpless before market developments that may not be in support of you.

22. Make an arrangement of trades

To wrap things up, consider making an arrangement of trades to decrease your risk. The portfolio takes a shot at any time allotment, in any event, for day trading. For instance, in the event that you've just taken three trades that are done in the US dollar, consider including a fourth trade that is contrarily connected to the initial three trades that you've taken (for instance, gold). This will counteract that solitary trades or a few trades do huge harm to your trading account.

Chapter Five

Top 7 Mistakes New Day Traders Make

Entering the universe of stock trading is unquestionably an extremely energizing time for some individuals. Most new traders are appealed by the possibility of profit in the financial trade. This sort of fervor can be an extraordinary help for new traders, be that as it may, it can likewise make them make some rushed, silly choices. At the point when individuals get occupied by the potential for enormous gains, they start treating day trading like a lottery. Trading isn't a lottery and stocks are not lottery tickets. You should never wager on a "hot stock pick" or go "all in" on a play. Trading is a craftsmanship that requires preparing and discipline. Achievement is conceivable. However, it is a procedure, not a moment of delight. In the event that you need to turn into a fruitful day trader, you have to place in the hours and work for it.

Here are the most well-known errors new brokers are typical wont to make:

1. Going in Unprepared

As referenced above, trading stocks ought not to reflect betting. You won't get rich by karma. Of course, a tad of karma can be useful. However, you ought to never rely upon it. You should be set up for the business sectors. The initial phase in readiness is training. You have to teach yourself about trading so you are appropriately prepared to ace the securities trade. You have to know how the market functions, what sorts of arrangements you are searching for and why, and how you will respond in a trade.

Going into the market, ill-equipped is hazardous and numerous brokers explode their records because of their hurriedness. Try not to get removed from the game that quick. Plan yourself so you can have the most noteworthy odds of accomplishment.

2. Absence of Proper Tools

Trading is a workmanship, and simply like any specialty, it requires the best possible instruments and assets. Take a stab at building a house without a sled and nails; it's not going to occur. In the event that you need to set yourself up for achievement in the securities trade, you have to ensure you approach the correct instruments. These instruments may incorporate intermediaries, exchanging programming, instructive assets, and that's only the tip of the iceberg. Ensure your tool stash is enough provided before you set out on your trading venture. You'd be astonished at how significant a solitary device, for example, a representative or stage can be. Do your analysis and ensure you have what you have to execute your trading plan appropriately.

3. Going in Too Big

You will regularly observe numerous parallels between new traders and players on the grounds that the financial trade and the gambling club both have a comparable intrigue. They offer you the chance to transform a little entirety of cash into a lot bigger one. The vast majority realize that they have low chances in the gambling club, in any case, very few individuals understand that they have comparative chances in the securities trade in the event that they adopt an inappropriate strategy. We've just referenced the centrality of readiness - this is the initial step to achievement in the business sectors. The following stage is legitimate money management.

Cash management is similarly as significant as trading methodology since it helps you secure your capital. It additionally gives you more pad for losing trades. On the off chance that you just utilize 10% of your capital for any trade, you can never explode your record from a solitary trade. 10% is a discretionary number, yet you ought to get the point. On the off chance that you go in too huge on plays, you open yourself to pointless hazard. Indeed, even a dealer with a 90% success rate has a possibility of exploding their record on the off chance that they bet everything. You wouldn't go into a gambling club and put your life investment funds on red at the roulette table (ideally), so for what reason would you go for broke in your trades? Ensure you are never betting and center around dealing with your cash appropriately. Of course, it's anything but difficult to consider the potential profits. However, you can't disregard the potential losses. It might sting a piece to feel like you could have made more on trade; however, it will sting altogether harder in the event that you explode your trading record and remove yourself from the game.

4. Following versus Learning

At the point when individuals begin trading, they regularly search for a tutor to gain from. There's nothing amiss with that. Truth be told, it's incredible to gain from the victories and disappointments of an accomplished dealer. The issue comes in when you attempt to imitate their prosperity through mimicry. That is the issue with a great deal of alarms administrations. They pull in brokers who just need to duplicate the careful trades of a fruitful trader. You ought to be centered around getting independent. When was the last time you heard somebody ascribe their prosperity to replicating a "guru's" trades? It simply doesn't work that way.

Gain from others, yet don't tail them.

5. Averaging Down

One of the most noticeably awful missteps new trades make is averaging down. This is an extraordinary method to transform a little loss into a record ruiner. We've all been there previously. You've just dedicated to trade so now you have a feeling that you need to finish. "The stock was modest when I got it at $5, so $4 is a take!" This rationale is imperfect and it will push you into difficulty. At the point when you normal down, you're adding to a losing position, in this manner delving yourself more profound in a gap. You're in an ideal situation cutting losses early. Nobody likes to take losses, however, assuming a little loss is far superior to getting yourself in a position where you can be removed from the trading game. There will be a lot of other trading openings in the event that you protect your capital. Have a trading plan and stick to it.

6. Not Cutting Losses

Not cutting losses is like averaging down. It will keep you down and possibly ruin your record. As referenced previously, nobody likes taking losses, yet it is a significant piece of the game. Simply think of it as the expense of working together. In the event that you clutch a failure, you open yourself to superfluous risk. That $100 loss can without much of a stretch go to $200, $400, $1000 and past. You have to know how a lot of cash you are happy to chance on a play and afterward finish it. It's critical to have the most extreme dollar sum that you are eager to risk. On the off chance that you ever lose more than that, you disrupted your trading norms. Be savvy about cutting losses early and you will have a lot more grounded possibility of prevailing in the markets.

7. Retribution Trading

There's nothing more terrible than attempting to compensate for an awful trade by setting more trade. "I simply lost $500, so now I have to discover a $500 trade to make it back." When you do this, you are trading wrongly and that is a catastrophe waiting to happen. You ought to never trade to compensate for losses. You should possibly trade when you have a prime arrangement and a strong trading plan. On the off chance that you start feeling like you are trading inwardly, step back and calmly inhale. You don't need to continue trading. This can help keep you from making a poor trade that you will lament over the long haul. Keep in mind; there will consistently be more chances to profit on the off chance that you safeguard your capital. Try not to get excessively on edge.

Chapter Six

Normal Investor and Trader Blunders

Committing errors is a core piece of the learning procedure with regards to exchanging or contributing. Speculators are commonly engaged with longer-term possessions and will trade stocks; exchange traded assets, and different securities. Traders for the most part, purchase and sell fates and choices, hold those situations for shorter periods, and are associated with a more prominent number of trades.

While traders and traders utilize two unique kinds of trading transactions , they frequently are blameworthy of committing similar sorts of errors. A few mix-ups are progressively destructive to the investor, and others cause more damage to the trader. Both would do well to recall these basic bungles and attempt to avoid them.

1. Lack of a Trading Plan

Seasoned traders get into a trade with a well-characterized plan. They know their accurate passage and leave focuses, the measure of money to put resources into the trade and the greatest loss they are eager to take.

Novice traders might not have a trading plan in place before they initiate trading . Regardless of whether they have an arrangement, they might be progressively inclined to stray from the characterized arrangement than would prepared merchants. Fledgling traders may turn around the course through and through. For instance, going short after first purchasing securities in light of the fact that the offer value is declining—just to wind up getting whipsawed.

2. Pursuing Performance

Numerous investors or traders will choose resource classes, techniques, supervisors, and assets dependent on a current solid exhibition. The inclination that "I'm passing up incredible returns" has most likely prompted more awful investment choices than some other single factor.

In the event that a specific resource class, system, or stock has done amazingly well for three or four years, we know one thing with assurance: We ought to have contributed three or four years prior. Presently, notwithstanding, the specific cycle that prompted this extraordinary presentation might be approaching its end. The savvy cash is moving out, and the moronic cash is pouring in.

3. Not Regaining Balance

Rebalancing is the way toward restoring your portfolio to its objective resource designation, as sketched out in your investment plan. Rebalancing is troublesome in light of the fact that it might constrain you to sell the advantage class that is performing admirably and purchases a greater amount of your most exceedingly terrible performing resource class. This contrarian activity is hard for some tenderfoot investors.

Nonetheless, a portfolio permitted to float with market returns ensures that advantage classes will be overweighted at market tops and underweighted at advertise lows—an equation for horrible showing. Rebalance strictly and receive the long haul benefits.

4. Overlooking Risk Aversion

Try not to dismiss your risk resilience or your ability to go out on a limb. A few investors can't stomach unpredictability and the good and bad times related to the securities trade or increasingly theoretical traders. Different investors may require secure, normal intrigue pay. These generally safe resistance financial specialists would be in an ideal situation putting resources into the blue-chip supplies of built-up firms and should avoid progressively unpredictable development and new business shares.

Recollect that any venture return accompanies a risk. The most minimal risk speculation accessible is U.S. Treasury bonds, bills, and notes. From that point, different sorts of ventures climb in the risk stepping stool, and will likewise offer bigger returns to make up for the higher risk attempted. In the event that a venture offers extremely alluring returns, additionally, see its risk profile and perceive how a lot of cash you could lose if things turn out badly. Never contribute beyond what you can bear to lose.

5. Overlooking Your Time Horizon

Try not to put without a period skyline as a top priority. Consider in the event that you will require the assets you are securing up in a venture before entering the trade. Additionally, decide to what extent—the time skyline—you need to put something aside for your retirement, a downpayment on a home, or an advanced degree for your youngster.

If you intend to aggregate cash to purchase a house, that could be all the more a medium-term time span. Notwithstanding, in the event that you are contributing to back a small kid's advanced degree, that is all the more a long haul venture. On the off chance that you are putting something

74

aside for retirement 30 years, consequently, what the financial exchange does this year or next shouldn't be the greatest concern.

When you comprehend your frame of reference, you can discover ventures that match that profile.

6. Not Using Stop-Loss Orders

A major sign that you don't have a trading plan isn't utilizing stop-loss orders. Stop orders come in a few assortments and can restrict losses because of antagonistic development in a stock or the market overall. These orders will execute consequently once edges you set are met.

Tight stop losses, for the most part, imply that losses are topped before they become sizable. Notwithstanding, there is a risk that a stop request on long positions might be actualized at levels underneath those predetermined should the security all of a sudden hole lower—as happened to numerous investors during the Flash Crash. Indeed, even in view of that idea, the advantages of stop orders far exceed the danger of halting out at an impromptu cost.

An end product to this regular trading botch is the point at which a trader drops a stop order on a losing trade just before it tends to be activated in light of the fact that they accept that the value pattern will invert.

7. Allowing Losses To develop

One of the characterizing attributes of effective investors and traders is their capacity to assume a little loss rapidly if a trade isn't working out and proceed onward to the following trade idea. Ineffective traders, then again, can become incapacitated if a trade conflicts with them. As opposed to making a fast move to top a loss, they may clutch a losing position with the expectation that the exchange will, in the long run, work out. A losing trade can hold up trading capital for quite a while and may bring about mounting losses and extreme consumption of capital.

8. Averaging Up or Down

Averaging down on a lengthy position in a blue-chip stock can be beneficial for a trader who has a long investment skyline, yet it might be loaded with danger for a trader who is trading unpredictable and riskier securities. The absolute greatest trading losses in history had happened in light of the fact that a trader continued adding to a losing position, and was in the end compelled to cut the whole position when the size of the loss got illogical. Traders additionally go short more regularly than preservationist financial specialists and incline toward averaging up, in light of the fact that the security is progressing as opposed to declining. This is a similarly dangerous move that is another normal error made by a fledgling trader.

9. The Importance of Accepting Losses

Awfully frequently, investors neglect to acknowledge the basic reality that they are human and inclined to committing errors similarly as the best investors do. Regardless of whether you made a stock buy-in scramble or one of your large long-term workers has all of a sudden gotten ugly, the best thing you can do is acknowledge it. The most noticeably awful thing you can do is let your pride take need over your wallet and clutch a losing investment. Or then again more awful yet, purchase more portions of the stock. as it is a lot less expensive at this point.

This is an exceptionally regular error, and the individuals who commit it do as such by contrasting the present offer cost and the 52-week high of the stock. Numerous individuals utilizing this check expect that a fallen offer value speaks to a decent purchase. Be that as it may, there was a purpose for that drop and cost, and it is dependent upon you to break down why the value dropped.

10. Trusting False Buy Signals

Breaking down of basics, the resignation of a Chief Executive Officer or expanded challenge are for the most part, potential explanations behind a lower stock cost. These equivalent reasons additionally give great insights to speculate that the stock probably won't increase at any point in the near future. An organization might be worthless now for basic reasons. It is essential to consistently have a basic eye, as a low offer cost may be a bogus purchase signal.

Abstain from purchasing stocks in the scratch and dent section. In numerous examples, there is a solid central explanation behind a value decay. Get your work done and break down a stock's standpoint before you put resources into it. You need to put resources into organizations that will encounter supported development later on. An organization's future working presentation has nothing to do with the cost at which you happened to purchase its offers.

11. Purchasing With Too Much Margin

Margin—utilizing acquired cash from your broker to buy securities, typically futures and options. While margin can assist you with getting more cash, it can likewise misrepresent your losses the same amount. Ensure you see how the margin functions and when your broker could expect you to sell any positions you hold.

The most exceedingly terrible thing you can do as another broker is getting diverted with what appears to free money. In the event that you use margin and your venture doesn't go the manner in which you arranged, at that point, you end up with a huge obligation commitment to no end. Inquire as to whether you would purchase stocks with your Visa. Obviously, you wouldn't. Utilizing margin exorbitantly is basically something very similar, but likely at a lower loan fee.

Further, utilizing margin expects you to screen your positions significantly more intently. Misrepresented increases and misfortunes that go with little developments in cost can spell fiasco. In the event that you lack the opportunity or information to watch out for and settle on choices about your positions and their qualities drop then your business firm will offer your stock to recoup any losses you have gathered.

As another trader use margin sparingly, if by any stretch of the imagination, and just on the off chance that you see the entirety of its viewpoints and risks. It can drive you to sell every one of your situations at the base, where you ought to be in the market for the enormous turnaround.

12. Running With Leverage

As indicated by a notable investment buzzword, influence is a twofold edged sword since it can help returns for gainful trades and intensify loses on losing trades. Similarly, as you shouldn't run with scissors, you shouldn't rush to use them. Novice traders may get stunned by the level of influence they have—particularly in forex (FX) exchanging—however, may before long find that over the top influence can pulverize trading capital. In the event that an influence proportion of 50:1 is utilized—which isn't phenomenal in retail forex exchanging—everything necessary is a 2% unfavorable move to crash one's capital. Forex specialists like IG Group must reveal to traders that more than seventy-five percent of brokers lose cash due to the intricacy of the market and the drawback of influence.

13. Following the Herd

Another regular error made by new traders is that they indiscriminately follow the crowd; in that capacity, they may either wind up paying a lot for hot stocks or may start short positions in securities that have just plunged and might be nearly pivoting. While experienced traders pursue the proclamation of the pattern is your companion, they are acquainted with leaving trades when they become excessively busy. New traders, in any case, may remain in a trade long after the keen cash has moved out of it. Beginner traders may likewise come up short on the certainty to adopt a contrarian strategy when required.

14. Keeping All Your Eggs in One Basket

Broadening is an approach to maintain a strategic distance from overexposure to any one investment. Having a portfolio comprised of numerous investments ensures you on the off chance that one of them loses cash. It additionally secures against unpredictability and extraordinary value developments in any one investment. Additionally, when one resource class is failing to meet expectations, another advantage class might be performing better.

Numerous examinations have demonstrated that most chiefs and common assets fail to meet expectations on their benchmarks. Over the long haul, ease record reserves are normally upper second-quartile entertainers or superior to 65%-to-75% of effectively oversaw assets. In spite of the entirety of the proof for ordering, the craving to contribute with dynamic chiefs stays solid.

Index all or an enormous segment (70%-to-80%) of your conventional resource classes. In the event that you can't avoid the energy of seeking after the following incredible performer, at that point, put aside about 20%-to-30% of every benefit class to allot to dynamic supervisors. This may fulfill your craving to seek after outperformance without destroying your portfolio.

15. Evading Your Homework

New traders are frequently liable for not getting their work done or not conducting satisfactory research, or due industriousness, before starting a trade. Doing schoolwork is basic since starting traders don't have the information on occasional patterns, or the planning of information releases, and exchanging designs that accomplished traders have. For another trader, the earnestness to make a trade regularly overpowers the requirement for undertaking some exploration, yet this may at last outcome in a costly exercise.

It is a slip-up not to examine a venture that interests you. Research causes you to comprehend a budgetary instrument and realize what you are getting into. If you are putting resources into stock, for example, inquire about the organization and its marketable strategies. Try not to follow up on the reason that business sectors are proficient and you can't make cash by distinguishing wise ventures. While this isn't a simple undertaking, and each other investor approaches similar data as you do, it is conceivable to recognize wise ventures by doing the examination.

16. Purchasing Unfounded Tips

Everybody presumably commits this error at some point in their contributing profession. You may hear your family members or companions discussing a stock that they heard will get purchased out, have executioner income, or before long discharge a momentous new item. Irrespective of whether these things are valid, they do not necessarily imply that the stock is "the following large thing" and that you should surge onto your online investment fund to submit a purchase request.

Other unwarranted tips originate from investment experts on TV and on the Internet who frequently tout a particular stock just as it's an unquestionable requirement purchase, however, truly is simply the kind of the day. These stock tips regularly don't work out and go straight down after you get them. Keep in mind, purchasing on media tips is frequently established on just a theoretical bet.

It is not necessarily the case that you should shy away from each stock tip. On the off chance that one truly catches your eye, the principal activity is thinking about the source. The following thing is to do your very own schoolwork with the goal that you realize what you are purchasing and why. For instance, purchasing a tech stock with some restrictive innovation ought to be founded on whether it's the correct speculation for you, not exclusively on what a common store director said in a media meet.

Next time you're enticed to purchase dependent on a hot tip, don't do as such until you have every one of the realities and are OK with the organization. In a perfect world, get a second supposition from different speculators or unprejudiced money related consultants.

17. Watching Too Much Financial TV

There is nothing on money-related news shows that can assist you with accomplishing your objectives. There are scarcely any bulletins that can furnish you with anything of significant worth. Regardless of whether there were, how would you distinguish them ahead of time?

On the off chance that anybody truly had productive stock tips, trading guidance, or a mystery recipe to make boatloads of money, would they yak it on TV or offer it to you for $49 every month? No. They'd keep their mouth shut, cash out their millions and not have to offer a bulletin to bring home the bacon. Arrangement? Invest less energy in watching money related shows on TV and understanding bulletins. Invest more energy making—and adhering to—your investment plan.

18. Not Seeing the Big Picture

For a long haul investor, one of the most significant yet frequently ignored activities is a subjective investigation, or to take a gander at the master plan. Incredible investor and creator Peter Lynch once expressed that he found the best speculations by seeing his kids' toys and the patterns they would take on. The brand name is likewise entirely important. Take a look at how almost everybody on the planet knows Coke; the budgetary estimation of the name alone is in this manner valued in the billions of dollars. Irrespective of whether it's about iPhones or Big Macs, nobody can contend against reality.

So pouring over budget reports or endeavoring to recognize purchase and sell openings with complex, specialized examination may work a lot of the time, however on the off chance that the world is changing against your organization. Eventually, you will lose. All things considered, an organization in the late 1980s could have outflanked any organization in its industry; however, once PCs began to get normal, an investor in typewriters of that time would have done well to survey the master plan and turn away.

Surveying an organization from a subjective point of view is as significant as taking a gander at its deals and profit. Subjective investigation is a technique that is one of the least demanding and best for assessing potential speculation.

19. Trading Multiple Markets

Starting traders may, in general, flutter from market to market—that is, from stocks to options to currencies to futures, etc. Trading various markets can be a gigantic interruption and may keep the fledgling trader from picking up the experience important to exceed expectations in a single market.

20. Overlooking Uncle Sam

Remember the assessment outcomes before you commit. You will get a tax reduction on certain ventures, for example, city bonds. Before you commit, take a look at what your income will be in the wake of deducting tax, considering the investment, your duty section, and your venture time skyline.

Try not to pay more than you have to on trading and business tax. By clutching your venture and not trading every now and again, you will get a good deal on intermediary taxes. Additionally, look around and locate a facility that doesn't charge exorbitant taxes so you can keep a greater amount of the income you produce from your venture.

21. The Danger of Over-Confidence

Trading is an extremely demanding occupation, yet the "learner's karma" experienced by some amateur traders may persuade that trading is the famous street to fast wealth. Such carelessness is hazardous as it breeds a lack of concern and energizes extreme risk-taking that may come full circle in a trading debacle.

From various investigations, we realize that most traders will fail to meet expectations on their benchmarks. We likewise realize that there's no predictable method to choose, ahead of time, those managers that will outflank. We likewise realize that not very many people can beneficially time the market over the long haul. So for what reason are such huge numbers of investors sure of their capacities to time the market as well as select winning managers?

22. Unpracticed Day Trading

In the event that you want to turn into a functioning broker, reconsider before day trading. Day trading can be a risky game and ought to be endeavored uniquely by the most prepared investors. Notwithstanding investment savviness, an effective day trader may increase a bit of leeway with access to extraordinary gear that is less promptly accessible to the normal broker. Did you realize that the normal day-trading workstation (with programming) can cost a huge number of dollars? You'll likewise require a sizable measure of trading cash to keep up a proficient day-trading methodology.

The requirement for speed is the principal reason you can't successfully begin day trading with the extra $5,000 in your financial balance. Online traders' frameworks are not exactly quick enough to support the genuine day trader; actually, pennies per offer can have the effect between a beneficial and losing trade . Most businesses suggest that investors take day-trading courses before beginning.

Except if you have the ability, a platform, and access to fast order execution, reconsider before day trading. In the event that you aren't truly adept at managing risk and worry, there are greatly improved choices for an investor who's hoping to build riches.

23. Belittling Your Abilities

A few investors will, in general, accept that they can never exceed expectations at contributing on the grounds that financial exchange achievement is held for complex investors as it were. This discernment has no reality by any means. While any commission-based shared reserve sales reps will presumably reveal to you generally, most expert traders and investors don't measure up either, and by far, most fail to meet expectations of the expansive market. With a brief period dedicated to learning and research, financial specialists can turn out to be well-prepared to control their very own portfolios and contributing choices, all while being beneficial. Keep in mind, quite a bit of contributing is adhering to good judgment and discernment.

Other than having the capacity to turn out to be adequately capable, singular investors don't confront the liquidity difficulties and overhead expenses of enormous institutional speculators. Any little financial specialist with a sound venture technique has similarly as great a possibility of beating the market, if worse than the alleged speculation masters. Try not to expect that you can't effectively partake in the budgetary markets, basically in light of the fact that you have normal everyday employment.

The Bottom Line

If you have the cash to contribute and can maintain a strategic distance from these fledgling errors, you could make your ventures pay off; and getting a decent profit for your investments could take you closer to your financial objectives.

With the financial trade's inclination for creating enormous gains (and losses), there is no deficiency of broken exhortation and silly decision making. As a private trader, the best thing you can do to cushion your portfolio for the long haul is to execute a sane venture technique that you are OK with and ready to adhere to.

Tips for New Traders

New brokers have various techniques and logical strategies to research and attempt as they approach the market. Below are some tips to help.

1.) Take Out Time to Peruse Different Types of Markets, Strategies, and Analysis Methods

Traders with more experience can return to the procedures they use, as well, and check whether they can change their way to deal with start turning a benefit. These are only a couple of options you can seek after as a broker:

- Trading penny stocks: Penny stocks are low-esteem stocks traded for under $5 per share. The profits are commonly low, but at the same time, there's less hazard since you won't need to invest a great amount in beginning trading. It's additionally conceivable to make a tremendous benefit in trading these reasonable stocks. You'll need to find out about over the counter markets and put additional work into examining an organization's money related history since organizations that trade penny stock don't need to meet the severe monetary prerequisites of the New York Stock Exchange or NASDAQ.

- Day trading: As a day trader, you'll open and close a few trades inside the same session. Since these traders are taking a look at variances inside a little time span, they're scanning for various signs of a decent exchange than long haul investors. Day trading is commonly not advised for learner investors.

- Putting resources into long-and transient techniques: You would someday be able to trade, clutch stocks for a considerable length of time, or locate a stock methodology someplace in the middle. There's heaps of adaptability by the way you exchange, and individuals have made a benefit utilizing different systems, approaches, and procedures in the stock trade.

Notwithstanding investigating various kinds of trading or procedures that might be more qualified to your character or money related objectives, you can take a look at various market examination techniques to give you an edge or put you on track to benefit.

The essential examination techniques are fundamental and technical. Both are utilized to foresee value changes and consequently educate which stocks to purchase and when. The thing that matters is that a basic examination takes a gander at the organization — its initiative, benefit history, foreseen increases, future objectives, notoriety, and so on — to check the stock's worth.

A technical analysis, nonetheless, sees market patterns and what drives financial specialists to settle on stock choices. You may discover accomplishment by moving your concentration starting with one investigation technique then onto the next or by attempting a blend of the two to educate your trade decisions.

2.) Trade in Dividend Stocks or Initial Public Offerings

Another choice for turning a benefit as a broker is to put resources into high return profit stocks. With this kind of venture, the organization delivers investors profits — a percent of organization benefits — each quarter. Financial specialists get a profit paying little mind to whether their stock has acknowledged in value.

Beginning open contributions are another decision. These are the primary stocks an organization ever offers, and however, most new businesses come up short, it tends to be an awesome chance to get a stock at its least ever cost. Since the organization won't have earlier benefit information, however, you'll need to accomplish more research about elements like administration and the organization's field-tested strategy and course before deciding if the first sale of stock is a decent risk.

3.) Perfecting Your Trading Skills

You don't need to be a specialist to make money trading, yet as you place more ventures and continue rehearsing and inquiring about, you'll normally show signs of improvement at trading stocks. On the off chance that you find that you're reliably not profiting on your trading — paying little respect to whether you're another dealer or have some understanding — you can pursue these pointers to help make something happen.

4.) Follow Some Stock Trading Best Practices

On the off chance that you find that your trades aren't getting positive returns, return to the inquiries you pose to assist you with picking an organization to put resources into. You may need to include or change the criteria you use to pick organizations.

You can likewise attempt some other accepted procedures for profiting in online stock trading, for example, putting resources into mid-and enormous top organizations. The previous have a market capitalization between $2 billion and $10 billion, and the last has a market capitalization of over $10 billion. Putting resources into these organizations is regularly productive on the grounds that market capitalization means that the organization's stock value contrasted with its extraordinary offers.

Another choice is to add an additional progression to your due tirelessness when examining organizations: tuning in to an organization's profit telephone calls. In the event that you've just evaluated the organization's quarterly profit discharge, this extra advance will give you a more clear comprehension of the business' authority and plan for pushing ahead.

5.) Monitor the Markets Every Day

Individuals beginning their first day of trading and those who've been in the business for quite a long time share one significant duty regarding all intents and purpose: observing the business sectors consistently. This will assist you with remaining over creating patterns, but on the other hand, it's vital to the time tested exchanging mantra of purchasing low and selling high.

Regardless of whether you plan on being a traditionalist, forceful, present moment, or long haul merchant, this general guideline should control your contributing choices.

6.) Buy Low and Sell High

Purchasing low and selling high is anything but difficult to recall, and it's a demonstrated technique for mesh a benefit as a merchant. In any case, you would prefer not to settle on motivation choices at whatever point a stock value climbs or dips. Truth be told, it's imperative never to freeze when a stock dips under the value you paid since the sum may bounce back.

To choose whether a sum is high or low enough to warrant an exchange, do this:

- Take a look at the organization's income per offer and representatives' buy action.

- You likewise need to take a look at the business' administration, benefit history, and life span.

You need to purchase low. However, you likewise need to put resources into an organization that will recoup — ideally directly after you've gained their stock.

A similar guideline applies to selling high.

In the event that you need to sell the stock so you can reinvest the benefits, you need to ride the flood of the stock worth expanding for whatever length of time that conceivable. The organization's prosperity may likewise imply that the business can reinvest in itself, which may additionally drive share value.

Persistence is thus important, however, you additionally need to know when a value is probably going to level or decrease. Following industry patterns and experts' actions can assist you with pinpointing the best time to sell.

In case you're keen on day trading or short selling, purchasing low and selling high will be imperative to your prosperity. You'll additionally be generally intrigued by unpredictable markets since frequent increments and declines in stock worth open the entryway for frequent gainful trades. There are loads of intrinsic risks, however, in unstable markets.

7.) Diversify

In spite of the fact that you'll, in the long run, become a specialist in a specialty advertise, a great arrangement for seeing predictable additions is to expand your portfolio. This is just prescribed once you have a strong comprehension of how the market functions and how to purchase and sell stock.

Diversification is significant since it secures you against industry changes. For instance, if every one of your stocks were in tech and an administration guideline or new development contrarily influenced stock costs in that part, the entirety of your speculations would be affected. A various portfolio is insignificantly influenced by such patterns.

This methodology is likewise a decent method to adjust high-risk and preservationist ventures. Putting resources into new companies is commonly risky, for example, since most are covered inside five years. On the off chance that you've put resources into a built-up organization in a specific industry, however, you can purchase stock in a startup in a similar section.

Their shared gainfulness could be all-around useful for the business, or maybe the greater organization will procure the littler one — netting you a sizable benefit.

8.) Reinvest

It very well may be enticing to leave trading once you've made a benefit. Nonetheless, on the off chance that you need to prevail in the long haul, it's shrewd to reinvest your income into other stock or into something less productive, however okay with solid, long haul benefits, similar to reserve funds or retirement account.

In Closing: Learn by Doing

To a novice, picking stocks may appear as though finding an organization that is performing great or searching for a startup venture flaunting an amazing item or administration and putting resources into them. For sure, a large number of the best stockbrokers bounced on great chances and left with tremendous additions. In any case, these individuals didn't fall in reverse into these examples of overcoming adversity.

Master traders carry their insight into the market each day. They realize what patterns to look for, and they recognize what makes a decent trade or awful trade — and when it merits disrupting their own guidelines. Certainly, a few people do luck out trading stocks.

In the event that you need to move unhesitatingly realizing that you can make cash exchanging stocks, however, you'll always have to be taking a shot at your methodology, watching out for showcase patterns, and standing prepared to strike at the correct chance.

Regardless of whether you're absolutely new to trading or have been bringing about certain losses and need to make something happen, probably the ideal approaches to succeed and make money trading stocks is to watch what trades specialists make and figure out how they're computing their options.

The key is to comprehend why the trade is being made — regardless of whether a pro isn't trading a region you're acquainted with, on the off chance that you can contemplate their philosophy, you can apply their methods and way to deal with your own subject matter. Truth be told, this is the ideal approach to figure out how to make money trading stocks.

Conclusion

I believe congratulations are in order because you have made it to the end of this book, and you have been equipped with the knowledge you need for effective day trading.

From what you have read, you would realize that the definitive objective of this book is to give you a superior chance to productively utilize the opportunities you encounter the same way a specialist trader would. Regardless of whether you are a regular broker that has lost a great deal of money before, this book will make trading quicker, simpler and multiple times increasingly productive for you.

And the sky is the limit from there!

www.ingramcontent.com/pod-product-compliance
Lightning Source LLC
Chambersburg PA
CBHW021446210526
45463CB00002B/650